Common
Aquatic Weeds

Common Aquatic Weeds

BY

L. W. WELDON
Research Agronomist, Crops Research Division, Agricultural Research Service

R. D. BLACKBURN
Research Botanist, Crops Research Division, Agricultural Research Service

AND

D. S. HARRISON
Associate Agricultural Engineer, Florida Agricultural Extension Service

with 116 illustrations

DOVER PUBLICATIONS, INC.
NEW YORK

Published in Canada by General Publishing Company, Ltd., 30 Lesmill Road, Don Mills, Toronto, Ontario.

Published in the United Kingdom by Constable and Company, Ltd., 10 Orange Street, London WC 2.

This Dover edition, first published in 1973, is an unabridged and unaltered republication of Agriculture Handbook No. 352, originally published in 1969 by the Agricultural Research Service of the United States Department of Agriculture, in cooperation with the Florida Agricultural Experiment Station, Florida Agricultural Extension Service, Central and Southern Florida Flood Control District, and the U. S. Army Corps of Engineers.

International Standard Book Number: 0-486-20009-4
Library of Congress Catalog Card Number: 73-76598

Manufactured in the United States of America
Dover Publications, Inc.
180 Varick Street
New York, N. Y. 10014

CONTENTS

Common
Aquatic Weeds

Introduction

Aquatic plants are rapidly becoming a major problem. A unique aspect of aquatic vegetation control is the great diversity of problems. Virtually everyone is concerned with aquatic plants because every body of water, as small as a roadside drainage ditch and as large as Lake Okeechobee, supports aquatic vegetation. Individuals may be concerned with the vegetation in a small boat slip or with maintenance of hundreds of miles of waterways. Aquatic plant control is important for all aspects of water use including irrigation and drainage, human and animal consumption, recreation, navigation, pollution, and public health.

Aquatic weeds are plants growing in or near water, which in excessive amounts are undesirable or interfere with the intended usage of a particular area. It is not uncommon for an aquatic plant to be desirable in one area or by one interest and undesirable in another. An example of this is where water lettuce is used as a decorative plant in a small reflection pond to add beauty to the area, while at the same time the vegetation is a favored breeding site of mosquitoes.

A number of methods have been used to control aquatic plants. Changes in the recommended practices of aquatic weed control have been common and will undoubtedly continue. There have been certain ecological shifts from one species to another, such as from southern naiad to Florida elodea in south Florida. However, such ecological changes are slow and usually cover a period of several years.

Recommendations to control aquatic plants can be found in the University of Florida Agricultural Extension Service Circular 219B,[1] or in the U.S. Department of Agriculture, Agriculture Handbook 332, which are periodically updated as dictated by current research.

The identification of the problem species is the first step in an aquatic weed control program. This handbook was compiled to serve as a basis for the identification of the more common aquatic plants. The various plants have been observed, photographed, and, where necessary, drawn to illustrate the more distinguishable characteristics. A description of the plant, its natural habitat, and its distribution and importance are included for each plant.

The plants are classified in five groups: Free-floating plants, aquatic grasses, emersed plants, submersed plants, and algae. Some of the plants could have been classified in two groups. The free-floating plants usually grow on the water surface and are not attached to the soil bottom; they may remain viable on moist soil for prolonged periods or be very loosely attached at the bank. Aquatic

---

[1] This circular can be obtained by writing to Agricultural Extension Service, University of Florida, Gainesville, Fla. 32601.

grasses are usually emersed, but a few species will also form floating mats. Emersed plants are firmly rooted on the bottom, but during normal growth extend above the water. Submersed plants complete their entire life cycle below the surface of the water, but may have floral parts above the water. Algae are a lower form of submersed plant life and are commonly called "scum" on water. The plants closely resembling one another and often confused are placed together within each classification to assist in easier differentiation of the problem species.

All measurements of length are in the metric system. The metric measures and the U.S. equivalents follow:

Length measurements [1]					
Metric measures			U.S. equivalents		
Milli-meters (mm.)	Centi-meters (cm.)	Deci-meters (dm.)	Meters (m.)	Inches (in.)	Feet (ft.)
1	0. 1	0. 01	0. 001	0. 039	-------
10	1	0. 1	0. 01	0. 394	-------
100	10	1	0. 1	3. 937	0. 328
1, 000	100	10	1	39. 37	3. 28

[1] Adapted from: HODGMAN, C. D., WEAST, R. C., and SELBY, S. M. HANDBOOK OF CHEMISTRY AND PHYSICS Ed. 41, p. 3137. Chemical Rubber Publishing Co., Cleveland, Ohio. 1959.

Free-Floating Plants

Water Hyacinth

Eichhornia crassipes (Mart.) Solms

Description.—Water hyacinth (fig. 1) is a free-floating plant distinguished by the bright-green, shiny, or polished-appearing leaves. The spongy petioles are often inflated and arise in a rosette from a central point. The petioles or leaves may be up to 12 dm. tall and may be partly submersed. The fine feathery roots are fibrous and branched. The inflorescence is a spike bearing several to many flowers that are quite showy and may be white, blue, or violet, with all shades between. The upper lobe of each flower is characterized by a yellow marking surrounded by a deep-blue margin. The plants reproduce largely by vegetative means and are interconnected by stolons. However, the seed will germinate on a flotant of decadent vegetation or on an organic bank or bottom.

Habitat.—Water hyacinth generally grows floating on open water. Plants can become established in very moist soil and then persist in a relatively dry site for several months at a time.

Distribution and importance.—This plant was first botanically described in Brazil and is thought by some historians to have originated in Puerto Rico. It was introduced into the United States in 1884 and through prolific growth rapidly became a pest throughout the Southeastern States. Water hyacinth has been reported as a serious water weed in most of the subtropical and tropical areas of the world.

Water Lettuce

Pistia stratioites L.

Description.—The most notable characteristic of water lettuce (fig. 2) is the light yellow-green leaves in the form of a rosette, with a tuft of long, unbranched fibrous roots extending from a central extension of the underwater rhizome. The leaves may be up to 6 dm. tall and are spongy and inflated. The leaves are softly pubescent on both sides and have several distinct nerves radiating from the base. These are more conspicuous from the underside. The mature plants produce a large number of small, inconspicuous flowers in the center of the plant. Seed production is limited, if it occurs at all, with vegetative reproduction mainly from buds.

Habitat.—Water lettuce appears to thrive best in still water or areas of minimal flow. It grows mostly as a free-floating plant, but can survive as a semirooted plant for prolonged periods. Water lettuce is not winter hardy and is often attacked by insects that are devastating.

Distribution and importance.—This plant is located chiefly in low-velocity streams and canals of Florida and along the gulf coast, with isolated locations across the Southern United States. It was first botanically described by Linnaeus in Ceylon, but was recorded for its medicinal properties in Egypt in 77 A.D. It is known in tropical areas throughout the world. An important consideration of public health importance is that *Mansonia* spp.

Figure 1.—Water hyacinth: *A*, Irrigation ditch entirely covered with water hyacinth; *B*, stems in foreground curved over into the water soon after flowering; *C*, closeup of flower.

mosquitoes prefer the roots of water lettuce to roots of other aquatic plants as a source of oxygen. Although large jams of water lettuce have been noted, the stolons are easily broken and water lettuce jams do not impede water flow and traffic to the extent of water hyacinth.

Frogbit

Limnobium spongia (Bosc.) Steud.

Description.—From a distance, the bright-green leaves of frogbit (fig. 3) are often confused with those of water hyacinth. The plants vary in size, and the leaves, which have a tendency to be heart shaped, extend from both long and short petioles. The plant may grow up to 5 dm. tall, but usually is much shorter. The petioles and roots extend from the nodes of the rhizomes in a rosette. The leaves are 5-veined and interconnecting veins may be visible. The petioles are somewhat inflated and are spongy. The white flowers are not showy and are found on peduncles generally about one-third the height of the leaves.

Habitat.—Frogbit is generally found floating in stagnant water, ponds, lakes, and marshes. It may grow rooted in mud, especially as a pond or marsh dries up.

Distribution and importance.—Translation of *Limnobium spongia* is "a sponge living in pools." This aptly describes frogbit because it lives in ponds and marshes. Frogbit is most common from central and northern Florida to Texas along the gulf coast and along the east coast to Ontario. Extensive growths usually create the greatest problems in the proper management of small ponds up to a few acres in size.

Water Pennywort

Hydrocotyle umbellata L.

Description.—The numerous leaves of water pennywort (fig. 4) are nearly round and are borne on a peduncle attached at the center of the leaf. The plant may grow up to 5 dm. tall. The leaf blade may be from partly to deeply lobed. The leaves arise singly from each node on the underwater or undersoil, slender, creeping stems. Small whitish flowers appear in umbels or heads and are

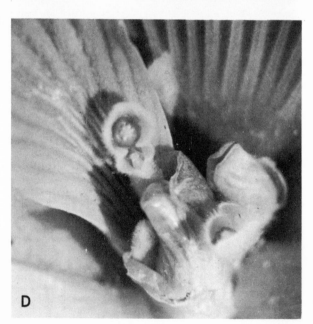

Figure 2.—Water lettuce: *A*, Large canal covered with water lettuce; *B*, mature plant showing vegetative offshoots, which are connected to mother plant by underwater rhizomes; *C*, horizontal view with the long, feathery underwater roots visible; *D*, closeup of flowers, which are found in the middle or crown of the mature plants. Note the distinct venation of the leaves.

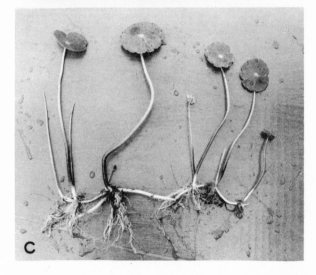

Figure 3.—Frogbit: *A,* Pond periphery covered with frogbit; *B,* interconnected series of plants; *C,* closeup of flower.

borne on stalks that may be as tall as some of the leaves.

Habitat.—Water pennywort is found rooted in mud along pond and canal margins and grows onto the water as a floating mat. Once the floating

Figure 4.—Water pennywort: *A,* Large canal covered with water pennywort; *B,* floating mat of plants with small whitish flowers visible in parted leaves; *C,* closeup showing underwater creeping stems and relative size of flower.

Figure 5.—Water primrose: *A*, Waterway infested with water primrose; *B*, closeup of plant; *C*, closeup of flower. Note the 5 showy petals.

vegetation becomes established, mats may break loose from the shore and continue to grow. Some species may grow equally well in either a terrestrial or an aquatic area.

Distribution and importance.—There are about 100 species of this genus in the world. *Hydrocotyle umbellata* is the most common species, but *H. verticillata*, *H. americana*, and *H. ranunculoides* are found throughout the Southeastern States. Water pennywort interferes with the flow and utilization of water mostly in small irrigation and drainage ditches and in shallow water ponds.

Water Primrose

Jussiaea michauxiana Fern.

Description.—The water primrose (fig. 5) is a perennial herb or partly woody plant. The leaves are generally diffuse and grow on creeping stolons early in the spring. The floating leaves found in the spring are ovate, but with the broadest portion toward the apex. As the plant becomes more erect during the summer, the leaves elongate and become elliptic. The leaves are distinctly veined. The roots usually are spongy and inflated. Flowering occurs from midsummer to late summer. Five yellow showy petals arise after the plant has become erect and is about 6 dm. tall.

Habitat.—Water primrose is found in ponds, slow-moving canals, and areas where water is stagnant. It usually begins to grow at the bank, but once a flotant has been formed, water primrose will begin to grow as a floating plant.

Distribution and importance.—This plant is most common in northern and central Florida and is also found in the Coastal Plains from North Carolina to Texas. The greatest growth takes place chiefly in small ponds and in areas with slow-moving water. Dead water primrose plants give rise to a flotant of debris that can support trees and other types of vegetation.

Primrose Willow

Jussiaea peruviana

Description.—Unlike water primrose, primrose willow (fig. 6) is always erect and has woody

Figure 6.—Primrose willow: *A*, Closeup of the primrose willow flower; *B*, mature plant growing in a floating mat of vegetation. Note the 4 showy petals.

stems. Mature plants are bushes 1.2 to 2.2 m. tall. Each flower has 4 showy yellow petals, distinguishing the species from water primrose, which has flowers with 5 petals. The woody stems are branched often from a central stem. The roots are generally embedded in a flotant of dead vegetation.

Habitat.—Primrose willow grows best in a slow-flowing canal or drainage ditch with a thick cover of other floating plants. It can also be found growing as a terrestial plant along ditches and canals and in other wet areas.

Distribution and importance.—The largest infestations of this plant are found in peninsular Florida, with scattered stands reported elsewhere along the gulf coast. It is also common in Central and South America. Primrose willow forms a flotant and eventually fills in the entire area. Primrose willow growing along farm laterals harbors insects and is a host for plant pathogens that may also affect economic plants.

Giant Duckweed

Spirodela polyrhiza (L.) Schleid.

Description.—The duckweed family, *Lemnaceae*, (figs. 7 and 8) has four genera; *Spirodela* Schleid., *Lemna* L., *Wolffia* Horkel, and *Wolffiella* Hegelm. This group of plants can be regarded as the simplest of flowering plants and some of them are the smallest. The various genera and species are usually identified by the number of nerves or veins on the leaves, which are actually fronds, and the number of rootlets.

The distinguishing characteristc of giant duckweed are its 5 to 15 nerves and 4 to 16 roots. The fronds are often purplish on the underside.

Habitat.—Giant duckweed (figs. 7, *B, C, D;* 8, *A*) is often associated with other members of its family, and is common in stagnant ponds and sluggish streams. As is true with other members of the family, giant duckweed is susceptible to wind movement. The densest growth in larger bodies of water or in streams is found among marginal grasses and other floating plants.

Distribution and importance.—This species is

Figure 7.—Duckweed: *A*, Pond covered with common duckweed; *B*, comparison of two duckweed genera, *Spirodela*, top, and *Lemna*, *left*, and salvinia genus *Salvinia*, *right*; *C*, overall view of *Spirodela*; *D*, closeup of *Spirodela*.

found throughout the United States and is reported in Asia and Australia. The greatest hindrance is caused in small ponds, which may become completely covered with a floating mass of duckweed several inches thick. Dense stands interfere with livestock drinking and may clog irrigation pumps. The mosquito *Anopheles quadrimaculatus* has often been associated with all but the denser stands of giant duckweed.

Common Duckweed

Lemna minor L.

Description.—The small fronds of common duckweed (figs. 7, *A*, *B*; 8, *A*) are commonly keeled on the back, are about 4 mm. long, and generally have 3 inconspicuous nerves. The fronds are generally grouped or attached in pairs. Some-

times 5 fronds are attached as a result of vegetative reproduction by the plant. A single root generally extends from a small pouch on the underside of the front. The very small flower is borne on a peduncle arising from the frond margin and this flower produces seed.

Habitat.—Same as that of giant duckweed.

Distribution and importance.—Same as that of giant duckweed.

Watermeal

Wolffia columbiana Karst.

Description.—Watermeal (fig. 8, *B*) is the smallest member of the duckweed family. The individual plants look like small globular particles of ground grain. The individual plants may be as large as 1.5 mm. across. The backs of the fronds are rounded. There are no roots. The flowers break through the back. Reproduction is mainly vegetative from a funnel-shaped opening at the base.

Habitat.—Watermeal is generally found in mixed population with either giant duckweed or common duckweed. Watermeal is usually found on or near the water surface, but may be found 30 cm. below the water surface. The plants may lie dormant on rather dry soil surrounding a marsh or pond margin, but will begin to grow again when the water becomes available.

Distribution and importance.—This plant is found mostly in the Central and Eastern United States and tropical America. It creates the same problems as other duckweeds.

Wolffiella

Wolffiella floridana (Smith) Thompson

Description.—The fronds of wolffiella (fig. 8, *B*) are rootless, up to 1 cm. long. They radiate from a central bud, often giving the plant a star-shaped appearance. The ends of the fronds are tapered and sometimes form interwoven masses. The bud or central portion is often nearest the surface of the water, and the fronds usually point downward. The fronds may point in any direction when the bud is slightly submerged.

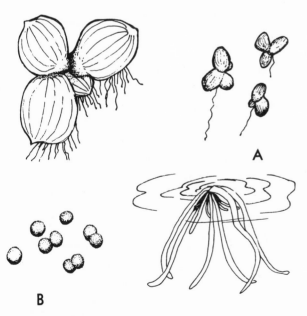

B

Figure 8.—Duckweed: *A*, Comparison of giant duckweed (*left*) and common duckweed (*right*) (3×); *B*, comparison of watermeal (*left*) and wolffiella (*right*) (5×).

Figure 9.—Azolla: Closeup of azolla. Note scalelike leaves.

Habitat.—The species often grows in mixed stands with common duckweed, but may also be found in masses of other vegetation, such as water hyacinth and alligatorweed.

Distribution and importance.—This species is found throughout the Eastern United States. It is chiefly a problem as part of a mixture with other duckweeds or other aquatic vegetation in ponds and stagnant water.

Azolla

Azolla caroliniana Willd. (Carolinian)

Description.—The azolla (fig. 9) is a small floating fern with small individual leaves banded together in a scalelike manner. The upper portion of each leaf is in the air and the lower portion is submersed. Rootlets are unbranched and inconspicuous from the underside of the leaves. Young or heavily shaded leaves are green and may turn red to brown upon maturity and more exposure to sun. The species is a true fern and produces sporocarps.

Habitat.—Azolla grows equally well floating on water or stranded on mud. It is generally found on the periphery of and in still waters. Vegetative complexes are formed with almost any other aquatic plant.

Distribution and importance.—This species is found throughout the Eastern and Southern United States. Azolla occasionally covers an entire pond or canal and interferes wih livestock watering and fishing.

Salvinia

Salvinia rotundifolia **Willd.**

Description.—The small, bright-green leaves of salvinia (figs. 7, *B* and 10) are arranged along a common stem, often with as many as 20 to 30 apparently 2-ranked leaves. In areas of sparse infestation the leaves may be found either in small groups or isolated. The leaf is distinctly midribbed, often appearing folded in the center. The leaves are 10 to 16 mm. long and are covered with bristle-stiff hairs. Sporocarps are formed on portions of the submersed leaves.

Habitat.—Salvinia grows mostly free floating in still-water areas. It appears to grow best in organic areas, chiefly in shallow, warm canals and ponds. Salvinia is often found growing in association with other aquatic vegetation, such as alligatorweed and water hyacinth.

Distribution and importance.—This plant was introduced into the United States from either Mexico or South America. The greatest populations of salvinia are found in Florida, but smaller stands are found elsewhere. It is sold as an aquarium plant throughout the United States. Small canals may become completely covered, which may be both beneficial and problematic. If the canal is relatively deep, a very dense stand will shade out submersed weeds that might have a better chance for growth with more sunlight. Thick infestations of salvinia float into pump intakes and have been known to force a shutdown of even the very largest pumps.

Floating Fern

Ceratopteris pteridoides **(Hook.) Hieron.**

Description.—Floating fern (fig. 11) is a floating plant with fronds 10 to 15 cm. long and deeply lobed. The spongy, inflated stems radiate in a

Figure 10.—Salvinia: *A*, Overall view of salvinia; *B*, closeup of plant; *C*, drawing showing 2-ranked leaves along stem and bristle-stiff hairs.

rosette from a central bud. One of the more distinguishing characteristics is the buds, which are borne in the notches along the leaf margin. These buds develop roots and as the plant approaches maturity, the floating leaves decay, leaving these small plants free for further growth. A spongy stem devoid of leaves grows from the central bud upon maturity. There may be several branches from the main stem, which reaches a height of 20 to 38 cm. The roots are long and resemble those of water hyacinth and water lettuce although the roots of the floating fern are generally smaller. Sporangia are produced as in all true ferns.

Habitat.—Floating fern is found in slow streams, canals, and ponds. It grows mainly on water, but has been observed growing on mud or moist organic areas.

Distribution and importance.—This plant is common in Florida and is found throughout the gulf coast. The species has also been observed in Central and South America. Pure stands of floating fern have not been reported as a problem because it generally grows in association with other aquatics.

Alligatorweed

Alternanthera philoxeroides (Mart.) Griseb.

Description.—Alligatorweed (fig. 12) grows as a mat of vegetation interwoven with stems that have become prostrate. The nodes generally have two buds, each of which may sprout to produce a shoot. Reproduction is by vegetative means from

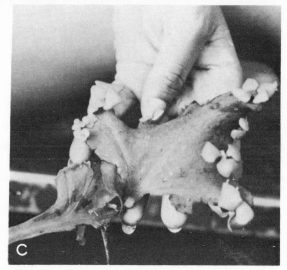

Figure 11.—Floating fern: *A*, Small creek covered with floating fern, alligator weed, and primrose willow; *B*, overall view of floating fern plant; *C*, closeup of mature floating fern leaf with developing plantlets on leaf margin.

Figure 12.—Alligatorweed: *A*, Large impoundment covered with floating and emersed alligatorweed; *B*, dense stand of plants growing along shoreline; *C*, closeup of plant showing round, white floral head and venation of leaves.

the axillary buds. The leaves are opposite, 5 to 13 cm. long, and lance shaped with a distinct midrib. A very few hairs may be found on the leaf surface and margin. The stems are hollow. Flowers occur in long peduncles in a solitary head up to 13 mm. in diameter. From 6 to 20 white florets may be found on each flower; each floret has 5 stamens. Viable seed has not been found in the United States. Roots may form at every node near or submerged in water or on moist soil. Upon reaching soil, the small aquatic roots enlarge, thicken, and in general take on the characteristics of other perennial terrestrial roots.

Habitat.—Alligatorweed probably grows in a wider range of water and soil conditions than any other plant. Equally profuse growth may be found when alligatorweed is completely free floating, loosely attached and forming a mat, rooted emersed, or in a dry field. Alligatorweed responds rapidly to fertilization; it grows best in areas of sewage inflow, fertilized fields, and similar highly fertile areas. Alligatorweed grows primarily in fresh water, but will tolerate salt to 10 percent of sea strength in still water and 30 percent of sea strength in flowing water.

Distribution and importance.—This plant is found in the coastal States from Virginia to Texas. A few small infestations have been found in California. Alligatorweed was introduced into the United States probably in the ballast of ships from South America. The greatest problem is caused in streams and canals where dense floating mats may block boat traffic and interfere with the flow of water. Alligatorweed often grows as part of a composite with other aquatic weed species, such as water hyacinth and water lettuce. Herbicidal treatment of water hyacinth and water lettuce may not control the more resistant alligatorweed.

Aquatic Grasses

Maidencane

Panicum hemitomon Schult.

Description.—The maidencane plant (fig. 13) has long narrow stalks with extensive creeping rhizomes, which often produce numerous sterile shoots. The leaf blades are 10 to 25 cm. long and 7 to 15 mm. wide, rough on the upper side, and smooth on the underside. The flowers appear as spikelets 2.5 mm. long, with the first glume about one-half the length of the spikelet.

Habitat.—Maidencane grows best in moist soils although at times it grows in relatively dry soils, such as cultivated fields. It grows along river banks, ditches, borders of lakes, and ponds, often extending out into the shallow water.

Distribution and importance.—This plant may be found along the Coastal Plains of the Southeastern United States from New Jersey to Florida and Texas. The plant may be seen as far north as New Jersey and Tennesee and as far south as Brazil. It grows well in open, grassy lime sinks and also in the Okefenokee Swamp. Of all the aquatic panic grasses, it is perhaps the most common and difficult to control.

Torpedograss

Panicum repens L.

Description.—The shoots of torpedograss (fig. 14) grow tall and erect from the nodes of strong horizontal rhizomes, which often creep extensively. The leaf blades are flat or folded, 2 to 5 mm. wide. The flowers develop from spikelets 2.2 to 2.5 mm. wide and 2.2 to 2.5 mm. long, with the first glume about one-fifth the length of the spikelet.

Habitat.—Torpedograss grows most rapidly and extensively along ditches and canal banks and in very moist sites. Growth along ditchbanks or canal banks may extend onto the water where large floating mats may cover a waterway. Torpedograss is also often found in terrestrial areas, such as pastures and groveland.

Distribution and importance.—This plant has been reported along the gulf coast from Florida to Texas and the tropical and subtropical coasts of

Figure 13.—Maidencane: *A*, Pond with encroachment of maidencane from margin. Note dense mat of duckweed covering the pond and intermingling with the maidencane; *B*, stand of maidencane growing in water 1.2 m. deep.

Figure 14.—Torpedograss: *A*, Drainage ditch entirely covered with torpedograss; *B*, closeup of plant; *C*, closeup of ditchbank, showing seed heads; *D*, seed head only slightly magnified. (Scale is in inches in *B* and *D*.)

the world. Possibly torpedograss is not native to America.

Sawgrass

Cladium jamaicensis Crantz

Description.—Sawgrass (fig. 15) is a coarse perennial sedge noted for its spiny, serrated leaf blade. The spines are hook shaped, like the teeth of a saw. Sawgrass is usually 2 to 3 m. tall. Leaf blades are 5 to 10 mm. wide with a fold at the midvein, and are more triangular towards the apex. Clusters of brown spikelets form along the culms and are separated by branches and leaves from the upper part of the culm.

Habitat.—Sawgrass grows in shallow ponds,

Figure 15.—Sawgrass: *A*, Overall view of sawgrass-dominant swamp in Everglades; *B*, plants growing along roadways through the swamp, showing relative size of mature sawgrass; *C*, closeup of seed head; *D*, photomicrograph of leaf margin, from which sawgrass is named.

pools, wet meadows, and marshes, and along canals and ditches in either fresh or brackish water. It grows equally well in water several feet deep and on dry ground several feet above the water table. It is rarely found at elevations above 30 m.

Distribution and importance.—This plant is famous as the dominant plant of the Everglades. It is also found along the Coastal Plain from Texas to Virginia. The very sharp leaves make travel through dense stands difficult. Sawgrass hinders waterflow and also creates a handicap in boat trails. Spicules from decomposed sawgrass on new organic soils frequently cause a dermatitis discomfort known as "muck itch."

Giant Cutgrass

Zizaniopsis miliacea (Michx.) Doell & Aschers.

Description.—Giant cutgrass (fig. 16) is an aquatic grass that grows to be 3.7 m. tall. It is a perennial with a creeping rootstalk. The leaves are flat, 3 to 12 dm. long, and up to 4 cm. wide, with a stout midrib. The leaves are smooth except for the very scarbrous margins. The large, open panicle or inflorescence is narrow in relation to its 30- to 45-cm. length. The panicle tends to droop or nod and has many branches.

Habitat.—Giant cutgrass abounds in swamps and shallow waters to depths of 1.8 to 2.4 m. Growth may also be profuse along creeks, riverbanks, and other waterways.

Distribution and importance.—This plant is found throughout the Southeastern States from Maryland to Texas and inland as far north as Kentucky and as far west as Oklahoma. Extensive stands are not generally found in southern Florida. It is also widespread in Central and South America. Large areas may be covered so completely that desirable plant species are excluded. The rank, coarse growth in an infestation easily cuts a person walking through that area. The mosquito *Anopheles quadrimaculatus* has been found in association with giant cutgrass.

Giant Foxtail

Setaria magna Griseb.

Description.—Giant foxtail (fig. 17) (occasionally known as giant bristlegrass) is a large annual grass 3 to 3.7 m. tall. Its scabrous leaf blades are generally 30 to 75 cm. long and 13 to 38 mm. wide. The stiff, erect culms do not usually branch. The curved or nodding panicles may be up to 38 cm. long. The panicle is crowded with branches. Each spikelet has one or two bristles 1 to 2 cm. long.

Habitat.—Giant foxtail grows primarily in wet soil in swamps and bottom lands, and along canals and ditches.

Distribution and importance.—This plant is found along the coast from New Jersey to Texas, in Arkansas, and also in the West Indies and Central America. The widespread infestations of giant

Figure 16.—Giant cutgrass: *A*, Large infestation of giant cutgrass; *B*, closeup of plant growing in water 1 m. deep.

Figure 17.—Giant foxtail: *A*, Growth of giant foxtail along canal bank; *B*, closeup of plant; *C*, closeup of seed head.

foxtail along canals with disturbed banks are the most troublesome areas.

Giant Reed

Phragmites communis Trin. var. *berlandieri* (*Fourn.*) *Fern.*

Description.—The stiff, erect culms of the giant reed (fig. 18) form dense, hedgelike obstruction along waterways. The culms are 2 to 4.5 m. tall with a large creeping rootstalk and may also have stolons. The leaves may be up to 5 cm. wide. The 15- to 45-cm.-long panicle is tawny to purplish and densely branched with spikelets. An important characteristic is the hairs that extend about 1 cm. from the florets and give the panicle a silky appearance.

Habitat.—Giant reed is found in swamps, along lake shorelines and canals, and in both fresh-water and brackish marshes. Giant reed establishes along the bank and may grow in water several feet deep or on soil with a high water table.

Description and importance.—Stands of this plant are found throughout the United States, except for a few of the Southern States, and are common in most of the world. The dense hedge growth along canals creates problems in normal canal maintenance. Giant reed often serves as a roosting site for birds. This has created problems at airports when large bird populations have interfered with air traffic.

Paragrass

Panicum purpurascens Raddi

Description.—Paragrass (fig. 19) is characterized by dense, spreading mat growth. The stolons are 2 to 5 m. long, but the leaves and culms are only 9 to 12 dm. long. The collars are densely pubescent with stiff hairs. The leaf blades are about 13 mm. wide and 10 to 38 cm. long. The panicle is 13 to 20 cm. long and rather distantly branched, with dense flowers on the branches.

Habitat.—Paragrass grows in cultivated or waste ground with moist soil. Growth generally begins along the bank and then spreads out onto

Figure 18.—Giant reed: *A*, Growth of giant reed along a large canal; *B*, plant growing along canal, showing relative size of mature plant; *C*, closeup of seed head.

Figure 19.—Paragrass: *A*, Floating mat of paragrass; *B*, closeup showing seed heads.

the water. Dense stands may develop into floating mats.

Distribution and importance.—This plant is found throughout Florida, in Alabama, and at low altitudes in tropical America. Paragrass creates problems in small drainage ditches where flow can be almost completely stopped.

Water Paspalum

Paspalum fluitans (Ell.) Kunth

Description.—Water paspalum (fig. 20) is also reported as *P. repens* Berg. in Small. (See "References," p. 43.) The culms of water paspalum are either glabrous or smooth; they are sparsely branched and sprawling on the water. Dense floating mats are generally found in early fall. The species is distinguished from other paspalum by the stiff, coarse hairs on the loose sheath. The leaf blade tapers at both ends and is 5 to 20 cm. long and up to 26 mm. wide. The raceme, or simple inflorescence, is spreading and rises 30 to 38 cm. above the water. Water paspalum is described as a perennial, but mats are difficult to locate during early spring. The mat apparently dies back each fall following flowering, then re-establishes either from isolated mats of mixed vegetation or from the bank in May and June, and then flowers in September and October.

Habitat.—Early season growth of water paspalum is most readily found along the banks in shallow water. It is a floating aquatic grass, forms large mats, and may be loosely attached or completely free floating. The largest infestations are usually found on rivers into which acid swamps are draining.

Figure 20.—Water paspalum: *A,* Floating mat of water paspalum; *B,* spike formation and branching characteristics; *C,* closeup showing smooth culm and hairy sheath.

Distribution and importance.—This plant is widely distributed in the Southeastern States as far north as Virginia, in Illinois, and in Indiana. It is mostly found in central and northern Florida. The large floating mats interfere with boat traffic and fishing on rivers and small streams.

Southern Watergrass

Hydrochloa carolinensis Beauv.

Description.—Southern watergrass (fig. 21) is a slender, perennial aquatic grass with a branched stem up to 1.2 m. long, which is creeping at the base and floats on the water. The submersed part of the plant is usually leafless with rooting at the nodes. The leaf blade is generally 5 to 8 cm. long and 1 to 5 mm. wide, is emersed only a few inches above the water, and is difficult to wet. The single flower spikelet looks like a miniature flag emerging from the carpet of grass.

Habitat.—Southern watergrass, which has a wide pH tolerance, is found in acid to neutral waters. It grows most profusely in the shallow margins of ponds and pools, and gradually encroaches into the deeper water to depths of 2.5 m.

Distribution and importance.—This plant is limited to the Coastal Plains from North Carolina to Texas and is not common in south Florida. Southern watergrass disrupts the harvesting of game fish in ponds and pools. The mosquito *Anopheles quadrimaculatus* is often found in the mats. Vegetative complexes with duckweed are especially common.

Figure 21.—Southern watergrass: *A*, Farm pond mostly covered with southern watergrass and duckweed; *B*, closeup of southern watergrass plant showing small blooms; *C*, closeup of floating mat of plants; *D*, plant in flower.

Emersed Plants

Spatterdock

Nuphar advena (Ait.) Ait. f.

Description.—Spatterdock (fig. 22) is a rooted emersed aquatic plant that arises from a thick, 5- to 30-cm., spongy, creeping rootstock. It is also known as yellow waterlily and cowlily. The leaf extends from the rootstock on a long stout petiole. The leaf blades stand erect above the water. The leaves are submersed or floating only during early growth or periods of high water. The leaves are commonly 20 to 40 cm. long and have a prominent midvein. The yellow flowers are usually 38 to 50 mm. in diameter and spheroidal with a small opening at the top. The flowers may be submersed but the ripening of the fruit is reported to take place above the water.

Habitat.—Spatterdock is often found in alluvial areas, such as pond margins and areas along rivers where water is shallow. Spatterdock grows particularly well in sluggish canals, swamps, and other areas where the rootstock may attach and spread. It may grow in water up to 2.5 m. deep, but depths of 0.9 to 1.2 m. are most common. In north Florida, depths of 2 to 2.5 m. are more common in large lakes.

Distribution and importance.—This plant has been reported throughout most of the Eastern United States. Extensive growths of spatterdock are established along river margins and in canals when waterflow is slack. This extensive growth not only further slows down this waterflow but also slows down fast-flowing water later. This all adds up to the silting problem in these areas. The plant spreads so rapidly that the waterflow in a canal is seriously curtailed only 2 or 3 years after the plant is established.

Fragrant Waterlily

Nymphaea odorata Ait.

Description.—Fragrant waterlily (fig. 23) is a rooted emersed aquatic plant distinctive for its sweet-scented, white, showy flower. The flower arises on a long peduncle and is open from about 7 a.m. to 1 p.m. The leaves, which are split to a

Figure 22.—Spatterdock: *A*, Drainage ditch infested with dense stand of spatterdock; *B*, closeup of plants. Note distinct midrib and manner in which leaves stand erect above water surface; *C*, flower, in center of figure.

Figure 23.—Fragrant waterlily: *A*, Large impoundment covered with fragrant waterlily; *B*, closeup of plant. Note distinct split in both the large and the small leaves that have just reached water surface; *C*, closeup of flower with white petals and brilliant yellow-orange center.

petiole attached at the center, lie mostly flat on the water surface, are green on top and often purplish on the bottom, and are usually 15 to 30 cm. across. The fragrant waterlily is a perennial with large, creeping, and often-branched rootstalks.

Habitat.—Fragrant waterlily has a wide pH tolerance; it is found in very acid and very alkaline waters. It is found most often in ponds and sluggish streams in water 0.1 to 2.5 m. deep.

Distribution and importance.—This plant is found throughout the Eastern United States. It is not usually a problem in the southern part of Florida. Ornamental plantings of fragrant waterlily in small ponds usually lead to dense stands that may cover the water surface. The greatest problems are in ponds and shallow lakes, where extensive growths interfere with boating and fishing and contribute to siltation as does spatterdock.

American Lotus

Nelumbo lutea (Willd.) Pers.

Description.—The leaves and flowers of the American lotus (fig. 24) are erect on a tuberous rootstalk. The leaves are circular, 30 to 60 cm. in diameter, with the center depressed, forming a cup or bowl even when it extends up to 1.2 m. above the water. The leaves are softly pubescent and are bluish green. There is no split in the American lotus leaf and this distinguishes it from waterlilies when lying on the water surface. The leaves produced early in the season lie on the water surface and as the petioles grow during the summer the leaves extend above the water. The leaf veins radiate from the center. The pale-yellow flower is about 10 cm. in diameter, with fruits forming in a spongy, top-shaped structure.

Habitat.—American lotus grows best in muddy, shallow areas, such as marshes and lime sinks, in 6 to 12 dm. of water.

Distribution and importance.—This plant is widespread in the Eastern United States. American lotus provides a favorable habitat for the mosquito *Anopheles quadrimaculatus.*

Figure 24.—American lotus: *A*, Large infestation of American lotus; *B*, closeup of plant standing erect above understory of alligatorweed. Note large lotus blooms; *C*, floating leaves. Note pattern of veins arising at top of petiole in center of each leaf.

Watershield

Brasenia schreberi Gmel.

Description.—The leaves and flowers of the watershield (fig. 25) arise from a slender, creeping rootstalk with considerable branching of the stems. The stems and the underside of the leaves are covered with a gelatinous material. The floating leaves are oval to elliptic, generally 5 to 12 cm. long and about 2.5 to 6 cm. wide. The stem is attached to the middle of the leaf. The underside of the leaf is purple; the upper side is bright green. The dull-purple flowers are borne on the peduncles 10 to 15 cm. long, with flower opening on the water surface. The identity of the fragrant waterlily (fig. 26, *A*), spatterdock (fig. 26, *B*), watershield (fig. 26, *C*), and American lotus (fig. 26, *D*) are often confused because of their similar growth characteristics. The most distinguishable characteristics are: Fragrant waterlily, leaves mostly flat on the water, round, split leaf with petiole attached to center, white flower; spatterdock, leaves erect above water, distinct midrib, yellow flower; watershield, leaves oval, gelatinous coating on underwater leaves and stems, purple flower; American lotus, leaves circular, softly pubescent, veins radiate from center, yellow flower.

Habitat.—Watershield is most common in acid ponds and lakes, generally in water 0.9 to 1.8 m. deep.

Distribution and importance.—This plant is found chiefly in the Eastern United States, but has also been found in the Far West. It is distributed throughout all but the southernmost part of Florida. The dense growths exclude desirable vegetation in small ponds.

Pickerelweed

Pontederia lanceolata Nutt.

Description.—There is some question as to the similarity of the two pickerelweed species, *P. lanceolata* (fig. 27) and *P. cordata* L., and whether they should be ranked together or separately. *P. lanceolata* is a perennial with a thick, creeping rootstalk that has clusters of erect leaves. Each stem has a leaf with a terminal spike of violet-blue flowers. The plants may grow up to 1.2 m. tall. The

Figure 25.—Watershield: *A*, Area covered with watershield and a few scattered large leaves of fragrant waterlily; *B*, natural growth of watershield leaves with small flower in center, riddled by aquatic insects; *C*, closeup of flower, several buds, and two leaves covered with gelatinous material.

leaves may be from 5 to 12 cm. wide and at least twice as long as they are wide.

Habitat.—Pickerelweed is found mostly in shallow water, including the margins of any body of water, and may completely fill shallow ponds and drainage ditches. It grows in a wide range of water qualities.

Distribution and importance.—This plant may be found throughout the southeastern seaboard of the United States. The greatest problems with pickerelweed are found where shallow ditches become clogged and lake margins covered. The vegetation interferes with drainage, utilizes water through evapotranspiration, and may render the water area useless.

Arrowhead

Sagittaria graminea Michx.

Description.—Arrowhead (fig. 28) is a rooted-emersed perennial aquatic with leaves 6 to 9 dm. long. The leaves are lance shaped and are from 4 to 10 cm. wide. The leaves grow as a rosette from the rhizome. Tubers are produced at the end of the rhizomes. The white flowers arise from the peduncle usually in whorls of 3, but there may be 2 to 12 flowers in a whorl. The flowers often extend 30 cm. above the leaves.

Habitat.—Arrowhead is found in swamps,

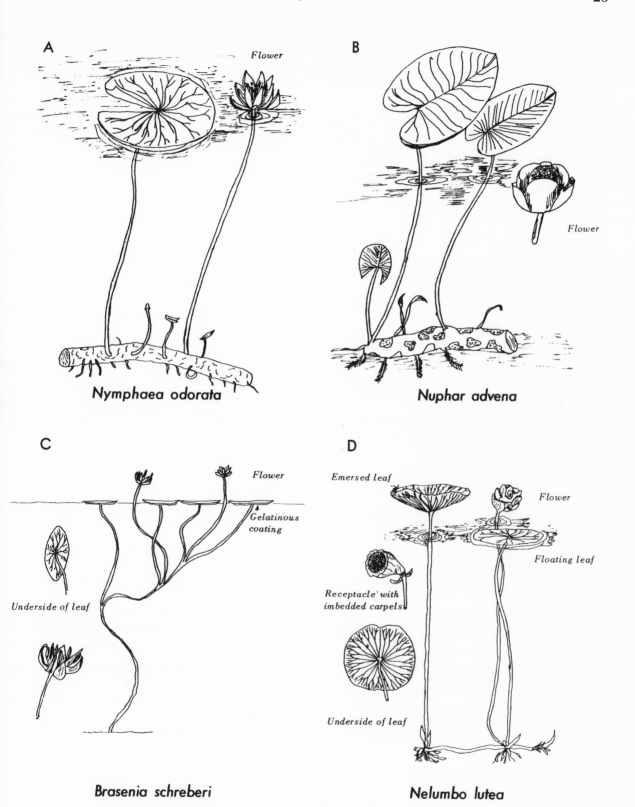

Figure 26.—Comparison of the 4 most common plants with pad-type leaf: *A*, Fragrant waterlily; *B*, spatterdock; *C*, watershield; *D*, American lotus.

Figure 27.—Pickerelweed: *A*, Closeup of pickerelweed; *B*, mixed stand of pickerelweed and alligatorweed.

mud, shallow water, and drainage ditches, and on sandy bottoms of lake margins and streams.

Distribution and importance.—This species is located throughout the Eastern United States. Several closely related species of *Sagittaria* are also commonly found in Florida. Arrowhead forms stands of undesirable vegetation in shallow ditches and lake margins where mosquito larviciding is important.

Buttonbush

Cephalanthus occidentalis L.

Description.—Buttonbush (fig. 29) is a plant also known as buckbrush but is most commonly considered to be a shrub; it has even been referred to as a small tree. The leaves are either opposite or in clusters of 3. The flowers are in round heads on the end of long, naked stalks, and this is where the plant acquired its name. As the fruit matures, it resembles small whitish-brown to brown balls, 2 to 5 cm. in diameter.

Habitat.—Buttonbush grows on moist banks of ponds and in shallow water a few inches deep. It has a wide pH tolerance and is found in the acid Okefenokee Swamp as well as in alkaline lime sinks. It is most readily found along edges of ponds and streams.

Distribution and importance.—The largest concentrations of this plant are found over the Eastern United States; however, the plant is commonly found in the Midwest and in eastern Texas. Buttonbush stands provide a favorable environment for the breeding of *Anopheles* spp. mosquitoes.

Cattail

Typha sp.

Description.—Four species of cattail (fig. 30) are found in the United States—*T. domingensis*

Figure 28.—Arrowhead: Drawing, with enlargement of flower. (Plant $\frac{1}{10}\times$; flower $\frac{1}{8}\times$.)

Figure 29.—Buttonbush: *A*, Buttonbush growing with other vegetation; *B*, white balls or heads of plant.

Pers., *T. glauca* Godr., *T. augustifolia* L., and *T. latifolia* L. They are tall, erect perennials with a jointless stem. The flowers are in a very dense, cylindrical spike 15 to 50 cm. long. The brown, dense pistillate is the lower portion and the staminate is the upper portion of the spike. The distance between the pistillate and the staminate serves as the basis for separating the species. The spongy leaves are flat to slightly rounded. The lower portion of the leaves are up to 5 cm. wide and 3.7 m. tall. Extensive rootstocks are underground.

Habitat.—Cattails are common in shallow bays, marshes, and all moist areas, in both fresh and brackish water. Growth is most common in shal-

Figure 30.—Cattail: *A*, Infestation of cattail; *B*, mature spike showing sloughing of threadlike floss attached to very small seeds.

low water where seedlings may become established in the mud.

Distribution and importance.—The 4 species listed above are found throughout the United States. Some of them are more localized than others. Hybridization has been reported between some of the species in Florida, and the species are hard to distinguish unless both the male and female flowers are present. Cattails may become a problem almost anywhere. They impede flow in small drainage ditches and may completely cover small ponds. Mosquito breeding is high in stands of cattail.

Softstem Bulrush

Scirpus validus Vahl

Description.—The softstem bulrush (fig. 31) is noted for its long, straight, nonbranching, cylindrical stems. The stems may be 3 m. tall and up to 2.5 cm. in diameter at the base, and gradually taper to the sharp, pointed tip. The stems are spongy and compress easily. The panicle is at the tip of the stem and has rather stiff branches. The scaly spikelet is brown.

Habitat.—Softstem bulrush is found in shallow ponds, along stream banks, and on lake mar-

Figure 31.—Softstem bulrush: *A*, Stand of softstem bulrush growing in water 1.5 m. deep and extending 1.5 to 2.0 m. above water; *B*, closeup of seed head borne at tip of stem; *C*, size of softstem bulrush compared with size of a man.

Figure 32.—Soft rush : *A*, Soft rush growing in small drainage ditch ; *B*, closeup of seed head of soft rush.

gins. It may grow in mud or in water several feet deep.

Distribution and importance.—This plant is found throughout the United States and tropical America. Large colonies of softstem bulrush impede the flow of water in shallow drainage or delivery canals when waterflow is low.

Soft Rush

Juncus effusus L.

Description.—Soft rush (fig. 32) is an erect emergent rush that is often mistaken for a grass or sedge. It grows in clumps of a few to several hundred stems, generally 0.9 to 1.2 m. tall but occasion-ally 1.8 m. tall. The clumps or tussocks arise from a short, stout rhizome. The culms are pale-green, round, 0.5 to 5 mm. thick, relatively soft and easily compressed. They appear to continue above the inflorescence. The whole inflorescence appears on the side of the culm about 8 to 15 cm. from the tip. It is pale brown with the flowers borne on a peduncle 5 cm. long, and the flowers are somewhat open in appearance as compared to a softstem bulrush.

Habitat.—Soft rush abounds in peaty swamps and prefers areas where it can stand in a few inches of water for prolonged periods. Wetland meadows provide a good habitat as do pond margins and shallow drainage ditches. It has a wide pH tolerance.

Figure 33.—Slender spikerush: *A*, Mass of slender spikerush along shallow water ditch; *B*, individual plant.

Distribution and importance.—The growth forms of soft rush are variable and the plant is said to be scattered all over the world. Often it is not included in lists of true aquatics, but it does cause problems in small drainage ditches by impeding waterflow and creating a suitable habitat for mosquito breeding.

Slender Spikerush

Eleocharis acicularis (L.) R. & S.

Description.—The most important characteristic of the slender spikerush (fig. 33) (often called needlerush) is the dense mats that are formed from the small stems. The circular culms are thread shaped, 10 to 15 cm. long, often branched, and with hairlike rhizomes. Spikelets are about 2 mm. long and reddish brown and solitary on the culm terminal.

Habitat.—The growth type varies somewhat with the water level. Growth may take place on either exposed or flooded mud. The culms tend to elongate more below water than when exposed above water. It is a common plant on wet shores and shallow water ditches. Shallow ponds with a variable head of water are particularly vulnerable to invasion by slender spikerush. The wide distribution indicates that a wide range of water conditions can be tolerated.

Distribution and importance.—Slender spikerush is found in almost every part of the United States, Mexico, and Eurasia. Dense stands are formed along the margins of shallow canals and these dense stands form mats of growth that completely stop waterflow.

Submersed Plants

Florida Elodea

Hydrilla verticillata (L.F.) Casp.

Description.—Florida elodea (fig. 34) is a submersed plant, rooted to the bottom, with long, branching stems. The stems may break loose and form floating mats. Florida elodea needs just a little light to grow and has been observed in water over 12 m. deep. The lower leaves are opposite and small, whereas the median and upper leaves are in whorls of 3 and are somewhat larger. The leaves are usually about 2 mm. wide and 11 to 13 mm. long. The flowers arise singularly from the spathe, and are found at or near the surface and from near the growing tip. The entire flower is inconspicuous and measures no more than 4 to 5 mm. across the tip of a threadlike pedicel. The staminate plants are rare; thus, seed formation is poor if it occurs at all. An underground propangle is formed.

Habitat.—Florida elodea is found in canals, ponds, and streams, particularly in calcareous sites. It is strictly a submersed plant and cannot withstand extensive drying. Large infestations of Florida elodea are found in drainage and irriga-

Figure 34.—Florida elodea: *A*, Canal with heavy infestation of Florida elodea; *B*, single plant showing crown, roots, and underground propagule; *C*, top part of Florida elodea. Note single small flower arising from tip of stem.

tion canals, fresh water ponds and lakes, and even in flowing or tidal streams.

Distribution and importance.—This plant is apparently found throughout most of the world, but not the United States. However, only recently extensive stands have become established throughout southern Florida, beginning in 1959 with a progressive ecological shift in canals and waterways from southern naiad to Florida elodea. Florida elodea interferes with waterflow and boat traffic.

Brazilian Elodea

Egeria densa Planch.

Description.—Brazilian elodea (fig. 35) is a submersed plant that appears to the layman as a larger version of the Florida elodea or another plant, *Elodea canadensis* Michx., American elodea. The general growth characteristics are quite similar, but with several key differences. The lower leaves may be either opposite or in whorls of 4 to 8. The upper leaves of Brazilian elodea may be 1 to 4 cm. long and up to 5 mm. broad and in whorls of 4 to 8, whereas the upper leaves of Florida elodea are in whorls of 3. Short internodes give a very leafy appearance to the plant. The flowers are strictly dioecious and are raised above the water. An important characteristic of Brazilian elodea is the 2 to 4 flowers that arise from a single spathe, compared with the single flowers of the Florida elodea. The white petals are about 10 mm. long, and may extend on the pedicel 2 cm. above the water. The pistillate plants are reported to occur, but

Figure 35.—Brazilian elodea: *A*, View of Brazilian elodea infection; *B*, closeup of plant. Note white flowers; *C*, closeup of plant in flower. Note two separate peduncles and flowers.

have not been reported as having been found in the Northern Hemisphere.

Habitat.—Brazilian elodea is found rooted to the bottom in about the same waters as Florida elodea. The larger stems make the plant somewhat less vulnerable to breaking loose, but broken branches will continue to grow free floating in water.

Distribution and importance.—This species is probably the favorite aquarium plant and as such is sold everywhere. Infestations could probably be found almost worldwide. Especially critical problems have been noted in central Florida, where several streams and lakes are heavily infested.

Widgeongrass

Ruppia maritima L.

Description.—Widgeongrass (fig. 36) is a submersed perennial with threadlike leaves. The stems are about 1 mm. in diameter and may be 2.7 to 3 m. long or be so short that the plants appear to be just a carpet of leaves 3 to 10 cm. long without stems. An extensive root system is found in the bottom mud or sand. The most important characteristic is the umbelliform cluster of fruit, with 4 to 6 fruits per cluster. Each fruit is borne on a stipe about 5 cm. long.

Habitat.—Widgeongrass grows mainly in brackish waters, alkaline lakes, ponds, and streams. The short-stemmed, low-growing type of growth is most prevalent in shallow water along the margins. The long-stemmed growth is most prevalent in waters 0.6 to 3 m. deep. It is reported that the habitat may influence the growth characteristics of the fruit and the length of the peduncle and stipe.

Distribution and importance.—This plant is widespread along both coasts of most of the United States and throughout Europe. The problems are mostly confined to infestation of small ponds but widgeongrass has been observed in drainage canals on Cape Canaveral. The seeds are eaten by waterfowl.

Common Bladderwort

Utricularia vulgaris L.

Description.—The stems of the common bladderwort (fig. 37) float just below the surface of the water and may be up to 2.7 m. long, branched, and leafy. The very numerous, conspicuous bladders are 1 to 2 mm. across and are attached to the fine leaves. There is an absence of true roots. The yellow flowers are borne on erect scapes 10 to 30 cm. tall.

Habitat.—This particular species is found floating in most fresh waters of Florida, throughout the United States, and Eurasia. It is usually found growing in mixed stands of aquatic plants in relatively still waters.

Distribution and importance.—This plant is found throughout the United States, but is less common in the Gulf Coastal Plain. It generally contributes to the overall aquatic weed problem of the area, such as impeding flow in a canal, since it grows in mixed stands with other submersed plants in canals and ponds. Mosquitoes are harbored in the foilage. The small aquatic animals, such as crustacea, become trapped in the bladders and are digested there. The free-floating nature of the plant presents problems in control as water or wind movement can obliterate a plant-free canal in a short time.

Vallisneria

Vallisneria americana Michx.

Description.—Vallisneria (fig. 38) is a submersed perennial growing from creeping rootstocks with fibrous roots. The leaves are clustered at the nodes of the rhizomes, are ribbonlike, up to 3 m. long. The upper part of the leaves may be floating on the surface. The leaves may be from 0.5 to 20 mm. wide, with several nerves and netted veins. The dioecious flowers are borne at the tip of a long peduncle, which coils and retracts the fruit below the water after fertilization.

Habitat.—Vallisneria grows in fresh water, mostly in lakes or very slow-moving streams not more than 3 m. deep. However, the exact extent of its adaptiveness to various depths of waters is not known.

Distribution and importance.—This plant is found throughout the Midwestern and Eastern United States. It is a preferred waterfowl food. The greatest problems are found in relatively clear waters where vallisneria interferes with boating and fishing.

Cabomba

Cabomba caroliniana Gray

Description.—Cabomba (fig. 39) is a rooted submersed plant with slender stems covered with

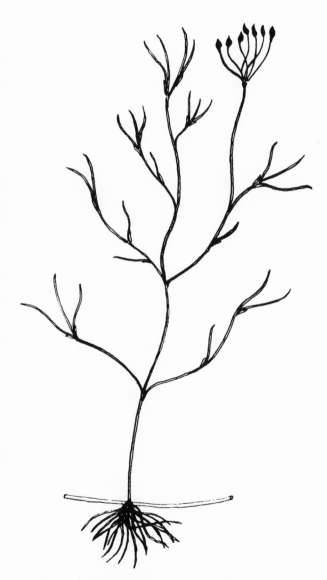

Figure 36.—Widgeongrass: Plant with proportionately enlarged seed head and accented sheath. (Plant ⅙×; seed head and sheath ¼×.)

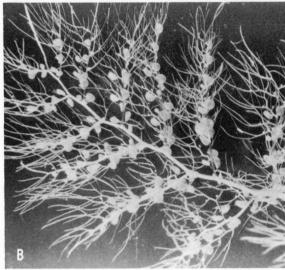

Figure 37.—Common bladderwort: *A*, Common bladderwort growing in canal, anchored at one end and free to move in current on end of long stem; *B*, closeup of many small bladders connected to stems and leaves; *C*, peduncle and flower arising from stem.

a thin gelatinous material. The leaves may arise from whorls or be opposite or, rarely, alternate. The leaves are threadlike and are finely dissected in the general shape of a fan 1 to 3 cm. across. There are a few small, 6- to 20-mm.-long, floating leaves attached to a long petiole. The flowers usually are borne from the same upper axis as the floating leaves. The flower is 12 to 20 mm. wide, with mostly white petals that are cream colored at the base.

Habitat.—Cabomba is most frequently found in ponds and quiet streams. It is generally rooted in water 1 to 3 m. deep, but may continue to grow after it breaks away from the anchorage.

Distribution and importance.—The largest infestations of this plant are found in the Southeastern States, but some infestations are found farther north. Cabomba is a popular aquarium plant and has become widely scattered by discarded aquarium plantings. Cabomba may clog canals and restrict the flow and normal usage.

Coontail

Ceratophyllum demersum L.

Description.—Coontail (fig. 40) is a submersed aquatic plant usually without roots, branched and with elongated stems. The leaves are in whorls and are finely dissected with a serrated margin. The minute flowers are found in the leaf axils, and are generally difficult to locate. The leaves are most crowded toward the stem tip, giving the plant the appearance of its namesake.

Habitat.—Coontail is most common in fertile waters. The unattached characteristic of the plant accounts for a diversified adaptation to fresh water.

Distribution and importance.—This plant is common throughout Florida and the rest of the United States. The largest and most troublesome stands are found in canals and ponds. Coontail usually is growing in association or mixed stands with other aquatic plants. The primary problems are the stream or canal flow impedance and the interference with fishing and boating.

Illinois Pondweed

Potamogeton illinoensis Morong

Description.—This particular species of pondweed (fig. 41) has a stout underwater rhizome. There are usually both submersed and floating leaves. The submersed leaves usually have at least 7 nerves, and may have as many as 19. The submersed leaves are slightly arched and are crinkly along the margin. The stalks of the lower submersed leaves are short, whereas the petioles of the upper submersed leaves are much longer. The floating leaves are somewhat rounded. The spike of the Illinois pondweed is borne at the tip of a stem, which may be 3 to 3.7 m. long. The peduncle is usually stouter than the stem and is 5 to 13 cm. long. The emersed spike is dense, cylindrical, and 2 to 8 cm. long.

Habitat.—Illinois pondweed is found mainly in calcareous areas in canals, streams, and lakes. It prefers fertile water.

Distribution and importance.—The pondweeds are widely distributed and there are many very similar species causing similar problems. Illinois pondweed is one of the species quite common

Figure 38.—Vallisneria: *A*, Closeup of small vallisneria plant; *B*, top view of vallisneria showing spiralling stems and small, inconspicuous flowers at tip of peduncles.

Figure 39.—Cabomba: Closeup of cabomba showing fan-shaped leaf.

Figure 41.—Illinois pondweed: Plant with seed heads that normally extend above water.

Figure 40.—Coontail: *A,* Coontail removed from water for photographing; *B,* photomicrograph of leaf margin of coontail.

Figure 42.—Marine naiad: Closeup showing triangular teeth on leaf margin.

in Florida, but not in other Southeastern States. Infestations of this plant hinder streamflow, impede boat traffic, and cause other problems common to most undesirable submersed aquatic plants.

Marine Naiad

Najas marina L.

Description.—The stems of marine naiad (fig. 42) are relatively stout, fragile, and branched. They may be several feet long, and are rooted to the bottom. The leaves are rather stiff, 1 to 3 cm. long, and 2 to 4 mm. wide; each margin has 3 to 12 triangular teeth projecting about 1 mm. The backs of the leaves are also often spiny. The leaves are opposite or in whorls of 3. The flowers are reported to be dioecious and the small seed is usually embraced in the leaf sheath.

Habitat.—Marine naiad is always found in alkaline waters, commonly in brackish ponds or lakes.

Distribution and importance.—This plant is very widespread throughout the United States and the tropical areas of the world. The most common problems with this species are the interference with fishing and fish production and the unsightliness of a severe infestation.

Southern Naiad

Najas guadalupensis (Spreng.) Magnus

Description.—Southern naiad (fig. 43) is a rooted submersed plant with slender, branching stems. The leaves are 1 to 2 cm. long and 0.4 to 0.8 mm. wide. They are deep green to greenish purple. The leaves are generally opposite or crowded into whorls of 3. The margins have minute spines.

Figure 43.—Southern naiad: Closeup of plant.

Figure 44.—Parrotfeather: *A*, Pond with parrotfeather, cattail, and aquatic grasses growing together; *B*, closeup of parrotfeather in water; *C*, above-water portion of parrotfeather.

Habitat.—Southern naiad is a fresh-water plant that will tolerate a slight amount of brackish water. Stands of the plant are common in ponds, lakes, and canals. Though the plant grows best in fertile waters, it also grows comparatively well in fairly nonfertile waters.

Distribution and importance.—This plant has long been the most common of the troublesome submersed aquatic plants in Florida. The recent ecological shifting from southern naiad to Florida elodea in some areas does not mean that southern naiad is no longer a major problem. It is widespread in the Eastern United States and tropical America. The greatest problems are caused by large infestations in irrigation and drainage canals

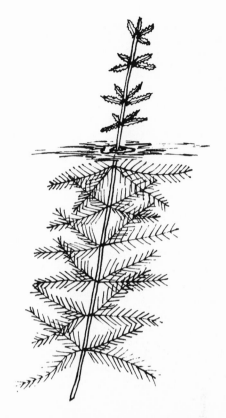

Figure 46.—Broadleaf watermilfoil: Line drawing showing serrated above-water leaf (¼×).

where dense stands may impede flow more than 90 percent of the designed capacity.

Parrotfeather

Myriophyllum brasiliense Camb.

Description.—Parrotfeather (figs. 44 and 45) is a perennial aquatic plant rooted in the bottom mud. The stems are quite stout and are sparingly branched. The emersed tip may extend 8 to 30 cm. above the water. The individual leaves are in whorls, generally 2 to 5 cm. long, and have 10 to 18 narrow segments on each side of the midrib. The above-water foliage is yellow and green, dainty, and graceful. The flowers are formed in the axils of the submersed foliage leaves. The fruit is 1.5 to 2 mm. long. Parrotfeather can also be classified as an emersed plant.

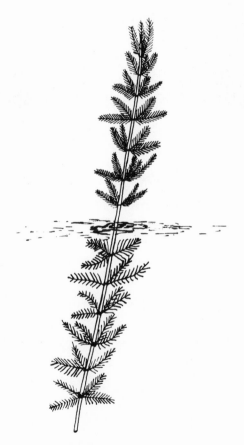

Figure 45.—Parrotfeather: Line drawing of parrotfeather (¼×) to compare with broadleaf watermilfoil (fig. 46) and eurasian watermilfoil (fig. 47 *C*).

Figure 47.—Eurasian watermilfoil: *A*, Closeup of eurasian watermilfoil plant; *B*, closeup of individual leaf; *C*, line drawing showing seed head above water (¼×); *D*, infestation of eurasian watermilfoil.

Habitat.—Parrotfeather grows well not only in aquariums and small fish ponds, but also in larger bodies of water and slow-moving streams. It is found only in fresh water and perhaps grows best in neutral or slightly alkaline ponds and streams.

Distribution and importance.—This plant is a native of South America, as the species name, *brasiliense*, denotes. Because parrotfeather is commonly grown in aquariums, its spread has been facilitated with escapes throughout the Southern and some of the Northern States. Small fishponds may become completely clogged and desirable plants and fish may be completely eliminated. Small drainage and irrigation channels also become clogged with growth of this weed.

Broadleaf Watermilfoil

Myriophyllum heterophyllum Michx.

Description.—Broadleaf watermilfoil (fig. 46) is a rooted perennial with most of the foliage submersed. The width of the stems varies from 5 to 10 mm., but they are generally stouter than those of other species in this group. The leaves are usually in whorls of 4 to 6. The submersed leaves usually have 6 to 10 pairs of dissected segments. The spike is emersed and commonly 8 to 15 cm. long, occasionally longer. The emersed leaves are 1.5 to 5 mm. wide and up to 2 cm. long. The margins are somewhat serrated. The fruit is formed on the emersed spike in the leaf axils.

Habitat.—Broadleaf watermilfoil seems to prefer less acid waters and is most common in ponds and shallow lakes.

Distribution and importance.—This species is very widespread throughout the country. It is not as common in southern Florida as in northern Florida. Large growths of broadleaf watermilfoil interfere with fish production and harvesting.

Eurasian Watermilfoil

Myriophyllum spicatum L.

Description.—Eurasian watermilfoil (fig. 47) is a perennial submersed plant that spreads very rapidly both by vegetative reproduction and by seed. It is rooted in the bottom mud. Each node produces roots, especially when it touches the soil. Large clumps of vegetation break loose and continue to grow even though they are not touching the soil. The leaves are in whorls and have 10 to 14 finely dissected segments on each side. The spike is emersed, 5 to 10 cm. above the water, and has no leaves.

Habitat.—Eurasian watermilfoil grows in fresh water but will tolerate salt to 33 percent of sea strength. The plant is generally found in water 0.3 to 3 m. deep, depending upon how much light is penetrating the water. It overwinters well in relatively cool water.

Distribution and importance.—Large infestations of this plant are found throughout the Eastern United States, with extensive stands reported in and near Chesapeake Bay, Tennessee Valley Authority Lakes, and Chatahoochee and Homosassa, Fla. There is no apparent deterrent to the further spread of eurasian watermilfoil. Thick growths affect shellfish severely, prevent fishing, interfere with boat traffic, and cause an unsightly appearance on the water surface.

Algae

Pithophora

Pithophora spp.

Description.—Pithophora (fig. 48) is an irregularly branched, filamentous alga. Initial growth is often made as an attached alga, but as dense growth occurs, gases are captured that form floating mats of algae. This floating mat often resembles a mass of wet wool. The individual strands are about the size of a thread, but are rather coarse.

Habitat.—Pithophora grows around small ponds and slow-moving streams and canals. It grows most rapidly during warm weather and in shallow water.

Distribution and importance.—Though this plant is found throughout the United States, it is most common in the Southeastern States. Dense growths of pithophora interfere with or prevent sport fishing, deplete oxygen, provide a favored mosquito-breeding site, and give an undesirable appearance to the body of water.

Chara

Chara spp.

Description.—Chara (fig. 49) is a large green alga, anchored to the bottom mud. It is symmetrically branched from evenly spaced, cylindrical whorls at nodes. The plants are usually encrusted with calcerous deposits that give the plants a coarse, gritty feeling. When crushed between the fingers, chara is ill smelling, emitting a musky odor similar to garlic or skunk. It is usually gray green, but may have a slightly different appearance due to the calcerous deposits and accumulated dead algae.

Habitat.—Chara is almost always found in clear, hard water. Normally the plant grows in shallow water but has been found in water 7 m. deep in a very clear canal.

Distribution and importance.—The many different species of chara require careful study for differentiation. The genus is found throughout the world wherever hard waters exist. The most severe problems are found in ponds and canals, where dense growths may impede waterflow and interfere with fishing.

Figure 48.—Pithophora : *A*, Canal covered with floating mats of pithophora : *B*, closeup of mat.

Figure 49.—Chara : *A*, Drainage ditch covered with dense stand of chara ; *B*, closeup of plant.

References

The following references were used freely to assist in the development of simple descriptions as aids in identification:

ARBER, AGNES.
1963. WATER PLANTS, A STUDY OF AQUATIC ANGIO-SPERMS. 436 pp. Hafner Publishing Co., New York, N.Y.
EYLES, D. E., and J. ROBERTSON, Jr.
1963. A GUIDE AND KEY TO THE AQUATIC PLANTS OF THE SOUTHEASTERN UNITED STATES. U.S. Dept. Int. Cir. 158, 151 pp.
FASSETT, N. C.
1960. A MANUAL OF AQUATIC PLANTS. 405 pp. Univ. of Wisconsin Press, Madison.
FERNALD, N. L.
1950. GRAY'S MANUAL OF BOTANY. Ed. 8. 1632 pp. American Book Co., New York, N.Y.
GLEASON, H. A.
1963. THE NEW BRITTON AND BROWN ILLUSTRATED FLORA OF THE NORTHEASTERN UNITED STATES AND ADJACENT CANADA. v. 1, 482 pp.; v. 2, 655 pp.; v. 3, 595 pp. New York Botanical Gardens, Bronx Park, N.Y. 10458.
HITCHCOCK, A. S.
1950. MANUAL OF THE GRASSES OF THE UNITED STATES. U.S. Dept. Agr. Misc. Pub. 200, 1051 pp.
HOTCHKISS, NEIL.
1964. PONDWEEDS AND PONDWEEDLIKE PLANTS OF EASTERN NORTH AMERICA. U.S. Dept. Int. Cir. 187, 30 pp.

1965. BULRUSHES AND BULRUSHLIKE PLANTS OF EASTERN NORTH AMERICA. U.S. Dept. Int. Cir. 21, 19 pp.
KLUSSMAN, W. G., and LOWMAN, F. G.
1964. COMMON AQUATIC PLANTS: IDENTIFICATION, CONTROL. Texas A & M Univ. College Station B-1018, 16 pp.
LAWRENCE, J. M., and WELDON, L. W.
1965. IDENTIFICATION OF ACQUATIC WEEDS. Hyacinth Control Jour. 4: 5-17.

LOPINOT, A. C.
1965. AQUATIC WEEDS, THEIR IDENTIFICATION AND METHODS OF CONTROL. Ill. Dept. Conserv. Fishery Bul. 4, 52 pp.
MUENSCHER, W. C.
1944. AQUATIC PLANTS OF THE UNITED STATES. 374 pp. Comstock Publishing Co., Inc. Ithaca, N.Y.
OTTO, N. E., and BARTLEY, T. R.
1965. AQUATIC PESTS ON IRRIGATION SYSTEMS. U.S. Dept. Int. Reclamation Bureau Water Resources Tech. Pub., 72 pp.
PRESCOTT, G. W.
1954. HOW TO KNOW THE FRESH-WATER ALGAE. 211 pp. Wm. C. Brown, Dubuque, Iowa.
ST. JOHN, HAROLD.
1961. MONOGRAPH OF THE GENUS "EGERIA" PLANCHON. Darwiniana 12(2): 293-307.

1962. MONOGRAPH OF THE GENUS ELODEA (HYDROCHAR-ITACEAE). PART 1. THE SPECIES FOUND IN THE GREAT PLAINS, THE ROCKY MOUNTAINS, AND THE PACIFIC STATES AND PROVINCES OF NORTH AMERICA. Research Studies of Washington State Univ. 30(2): 19-14.
SMALL, J. K.
1933. MANUAL OF THE SOUTHEASTERN FLORA. 1554 pp. Univ. of North Carolina Press, Chapel Hill, N.C.
U.S. DEPT. of AGRICULTURE.
1948. YEARBOOK OF AGRICULTURE: GRASS. 892 pp. U.S. Government Printing Office, Washington, D.C.
WELDON, L. W., and BLACKBURN, R. D.
1962. IDENTIFICATION OF COMMON AQUATIC WEEDS. Hyacinth Control Jour. 1: 32-37.
WILD, HIRAM.
1961. HARMFUL AQUATIC PLANTS IN AFRICA AND MADA-GASCAR. Sci. Council for Africa South of the Sahara Pub. 73, 68 pp.

**A CATALOGUE OF SELECTED DOVER BOOKS
IN ALL FIELDS OF INTEREST**

A CATALOGUE OF SELECTED DOVER BOOKS
IN ALL FIELDS OF INTEREST

AMERICA'S OLD MASTERS, James T. Flexner. Four men emerged unexpectedly from provincial 18th century America to leadership in European art: Benjamin West, J. S. Copley, C. R. Peale, Gilbert Stuart. Brilliant coverage of lives and contributions. Revised, 1967 edition. 69 plates. 365pp. of text.

21806-6 Paperbound $3.00

FIRST FLOWERS OF OUR WILDERNESS: AMERICAN PAINTING, THE COLONIAL PERIOD, James T. Flexner. Painters, and regional painting traditions from earliest Colonial times up to the emergence of Copley, West and Peale Sr., Foster, Gustavus Hesselius, Feke, John Smibert and many anonymous painters in the primitive manner. Engaging presentation, with 162 illustrations. xxii + 368pp.

22180-6 Paperbound $3.50

THE LIGHT OF DISTANT SKIES: AMERICAN PAINTING, 1760-1835, James T. Flexner. The great generation of early American painters goes to Europe to learn and to teach: West, Copley, Gilbert Stuart and others. Allston, Trumbull, Morse; also contemporary American painters—primitives, derivatives, academics—who remained in America. 102 illustrations. xiii + 306pp. 22179-2 Paperbound $3.50

A HISTORY OF THE RISE AND PROGRESS OF THE ARTS OF DESIGN IN THE UNITED STATES, William Dunlap. Much the richest mine of information on early American painters, sculptors, architects, engravers, miniaturists, etc. The only source of information for scores of artists, the major primary source for many others. Unabridged reprint of rare original 1834 edition, with new introduction by James T. Flexner, and 394 new illustrations. Edited by Rita Weiss. 6⅝ x 9⅝.

21695-0, 21696-9, 21697-7 Three volumes, Paperbound $13.50

EPOCHS OF CHINESE AND JAPANESE ART, Ernest F. Fenollosa. From primitive Chinese art to the 20th century, thorough history, explanation of every important art period and form, including Japanese woodcuts; main stress on China and Japan, but Tibet, Korea also included. Still unexcelled for its detailed, rich coverage of cultural background, aesthetic elements, diffusion studies, particularly of the historical period. 2nd, 1913 edition. 242 illustrations. lii + 439pp. of text.

20364-6, 20365-4 Two volumes, Paperbound $6.00

THE GENTLE ART OF MAKING ENEMIES, James A. M. Whistler. Greatest wit of his day deflates Oscar Wilde, Ruskin, Swinburne; strikes back at inane critics, exhibitions, art journalism; aesthetics of impressionist revolution in most striking form. Highly readable classic by great painter. Reproduction of edition designed by Whistler. Introduction by Alfred Werner. xxxvi + 334pp.

21875-9 Paperbound $2.50

VISUAL ILLUSIONS: THEIR CAUSES, CHARACTERISTICS, AND APPLICATIONS, Matthew Luckiesh. Thorough description and discussion of optical illusion, geometric and perspective, particularly; size and shape distortions, illusions of color, of motion; natural illusions; use of illusion in art and magic, industry, etc. Most useful today with op art, also for classical art. Scores of effects illustrated. Introduction by William H. Ittleson. 100 illustrations. xxi + 252pp.

21530-X Paperbound $2.00

A HANDBOOK OF ANATOMY FOR ART STUDENTS, Arthur Thomson. Thorough, virtually exhaustive coverage of skeletal structure, musculature, etc. Full text, supplemented by anatomical diagrams and drawings and by photographs of undraped figures. Unique in its comparison of male and female forms, pointing out differences of contour, texture, form. 211 figures, 40 drawings, 86 photographs. xx + 459pp. 5⅜ x 8⅜. 21163-0 Paperbound $3.50

150 MASTERPIECES OF DRAWING, Selected by Anthony Toney. Full page reproductions of drawings from the early 16th to the end of the 18th century, all beautifully reproduced: Rembrandt, Michelangelo, Dürer, Fragonard, Urs, Graf, Wouwerman, many others. First-rate browsing book, model book for artists. xviii + 150pp. 8⅜ x 11¼. 21032-4 Paperbound $2.50

THE LATER WORK OF AUBREY BEARDSLEY, Aubrey Beardsley. Exotic, erotic, ironic masterpieces in full maturity: Comedy Ballet, Venus and Tannhauser, Pierrot, Lysistrata, Rape of the Lock, Savoy material, Ali Baba, Volpone, etc. This material revolutionized the art world, and is still powerful, fresh, brilliant. With *The Early Work*, all Beardsley's finest work. 174 plates, 2 in color. xiv + 176pp. 8⅛ x 11.

21817-1 Paperbound $3.00

DRAWINGS OF REMBRANDT, Rembrandt van Rijn. Complete reproduction of fabulously rare edition by Lippmann and Hofstede de Groot, completely reedited, updated, improved by Prof. Seymour Slive, Fogg Museum. Portraits, Biblical sketches, landscapes, Oriental types, nudes, episodes from classical mythology—All Rembrandt's fertile genius. Also selection of drawings by his pupils and followers. "Stunning volumes," *Saturday Review*. 550 illustrations. lxxviii + 552pp. 9⅛ x 12¼. 21485-0, 21486-9 Two volumes, Paperbound $10.00

THE DISASTERS OF WAR, Francisco Goya. One of the masterpieces of Western civilization—83 etchings that record Goya's shattering, bitter reaction to the Napoleonic war that swept through Spain after the insurrection of 1808 and to war in general. Reprint of the first edition, with three additional plates from Boston's Museum of Fine Arts. All plates facsimile size. Introduction by Philip Hofer, Fogg Museum. v + 97pp. 9⅜ x 8¼. 21872-4 Paperbound $2.00

GRAPHIC WORKS OF ODILON REDON. Largest collection of Redon's graphic works ever assembled: 172 lithographs, 28 etchings and engravings, 9 drawings. These include some of his most famous works. All the plates from *Odilon Redon: oeuvre graphique complet,* plus additional plates. New introduction and caption translations by Alfred Werner. 209 illustrations. xxvii + 209pp. 9⅛ x 12¼.

21966-8 Paperbound $4.00

DESIGN BY ACCIDENT; A BOOK OF "ACCIDENTAL EFFECTS" FOR ARTISTS AND DESIGNERS, James F. O'Brien. Create your own unique, striking, imaginative effects by "controlled accident" interaction of materials: paints and lacquers, oil and water based paints, splatter, crackling materials, shatter, similar items. Everything you do will be different; first book on this limitless art, so useful to both fine artist and commercial artist. Full instructions. 192 plates showing "accidents," 8 in color. viii + 215pp. 8⅜ x 11¼.　　　　　　　　　　　　21942-9 Paperbound $3.50

THE BOOK OF SIGNS, Rudolf Koch. Famed German type designer draws 493 beautiful symbols: religious, mystical, alchemical, imperial, property marks, runes, etc. Remarkable fusion of traditional and modern. Good for suggestions of timelessness, smartness, modernity. Text. vi + 104pp. 6⅛ x 9¼.
　　　　　　　　　　　　　　　　　　20162-7 Paperbound $1.25

HISTORY OF INDIAN AND INDONESIAN ART, Ananda K. Coomaraswamy. An unabridged republication of one of the finest books by a great scholar in Eastern art. Rich in descriptive material, history, social backgrounds; Sunga reliefs, Rajput paintings, Gupta temples, Burmese frescoes, textiles, jewelry, sculpture, etc. 400 photos. viii + 423pp. 6⅜ x 9¾.　　　　　　　21436-2 Paperbound $5.00

PRIMITIVE ART, Franz Boas. America's foremost anthropologist surveys textiles, ceramics, woodcarving, basketry, metalwork, etc.; patterns, technology, creation of symbols, style origins. All areas of world, but very full on Northwest Coast Indians. More than 350 illustrations of baskets, boxes, totem poles, weapons, etc. 378 pp.
　　　　　　　　　　　　　　　　　　20025-6 Paperbound $3.00

THE GENTLEMAN AND CABINET MAKER'S DIRECTOR, Thomas Chippendale. Full reprint (third edition, 1762) of most influential furniture book of all time, by master cabinetmaker. 200 plates, illustrating chairs, sofas, mirrors, tables, cabinets, plus 24 photographs of surviving pieces. Biographical introduction by N. Bienenstock. vi + 249pp. 9⅞ x 12¾.　　　　　　　21601-2 Paperbound $4.00

AMERICAN ANTIQUE FURNITURE, Edgar G. Miller, Jr. The basic coverage of all American furniture before 1840. Individual chapters cover type of furniture—clocks, tables, sideboards, etc.—chronologically, with inexhaustible wealth of data. More than 2100 photographs, all identified, commented on. Essential to all early American collectors. Introduction by H. E. Keyes. vi + 1106pp. 7⅞ x 10¾.
　　　　　　21599-7, 21600-4 Two volumes, Paperbound $11.00

PENNSYLVANIA DUTCH AMERICAN FOLK ART, Henry J. Kauffman. 279 photos, 28 drawings of tulipware, Fraktur script, painted tinware, toys, flowered furniture, quilts, samplers, hex signs, house interiors, etc. Full descriptive text. Excellent for tourist, rewarding for designer, collector. Map. 146pp. 7⅞ x 10¾.
　　　　　　　　　　　　　　　　　　21205-X Paperbound $2.50

EARLY NEW ENGLAND GRAVESTONE RUBBINGS, Edmund V. Gillon, Jr. 43 photographs, 226 carefully reproduced rubbings show heavily symbolic, sometimes macabre early gravestones, up to early 19th century. Remarkable early American primitive art, occasionally strikingly beautiful; always powerful. Text. xxvi + 207pp. 8⅜ x 11¼.　　　　　　　　　　　　21380-3 Paperbound $3.50

ALPHABETS AND ORNAMENTS, Ernst Lehner. Well-known pictorial source for decorative alphabets, script examples, cartouches, frames, decorative title pages, calligraphic initials, borders, similar material. 14th to 19th century, mostly European. Useful in almost any graphic arts designing, varied styles. 750 illustrations. 256pp. 7 x 10.   21905-4 Paperbound $4.00

PAINTING: A CREATIVE APPROACH, Norman Colquhoun. For the beginner simple guide provides an instructive approach to painting: major stumbling blocks for beginner; overcoming them, technical points; paints and pigments; oil painting; watercolor and other media and color. New section on "plastic" paints. Glossary. Formerly *Paint Your Own Pictures*. 221pp.   22000-1 Paperbound $1.75

THE ENJOYMENT AND USE OF COLOR, Walter Sargent. Explanation of the relations between colors themselves and between colors in nature and art, including hundreds of little-known facts about color values, intensities, effects of high and low illumination, complementary colors. Many practical hints for painters, references to great masters. 7 color plates, 29 illustrations. x + 274pp.
20944-X Paperbound $2.75

THE NOTEBOOKS OF LEONARDO DA VINCI, compiled and edited by Jean Paul Richter. 1566 extracts from original manuscripts reveal the full range of Leonardo's versatile genius: all his writings on painting, sculpture, architecture, anatomy, astronomy, geography, topography, physiology, mining, music, etc., in both Italian and English, with 186 plates of manuscript pages and more than 500 additional drawings. Includes studies for the Last Supper, the lost Sforza monument, and other works. Total of xlvii + 866pp. 7⅞ x 10¾.
22572-0, 22573-9 Two volumes, Paperbound $10.00

MONTGOMERY WARD CATALOGUE OF 1895. Tea gowns, yards of flannel and pillow-case lace, stereoscopes, books of gospel hymns, the New Improved Singer Sewing Machine, side saddles, milk skimmers, straight-edged razors, high-button shoes, spittoons, and on and on . . . listing some 25,000 items, practically all illustrated. Essential to the shoppers of the 1890's, it is our truest record of the spirit of the period. Unaltered reprint of Issue No. 57, Spring and Summer 1895. Introduction by Boris Emmet. Innumerable illustrations. xiii + 624pp. 8½ x 11⅝.
22377-9 Paperbound $6.95

THE CRYSTAL PALACE EXHIBITION ILLUSTRATED CATALOGUE (LONDON, 1851). One of the wonders of the modern world—the Crystal Palace Exhibition in which all the nations of the civilized world exhibited their achievements in the arts and sciences—presented in an equally important illustrated catalogue. More than 1700 items pictured with accompanying text—ceramics, textiles, cast-iron work, carpets, pianos, sleds, razors, wall-papers, billiard tables, beehives, silverware and hundreds of other artifacts—represent the focal point of Victorian culture in the Western World. Probably the largest collection of Victorian decorative art ever assembled—indispensable for antiquarians and designers. Unabridged republication of the Art-Journal Catalogue of the Great Exhibition of 1851, with all terminal essays. New introduction by John Gloag, F.S.A. xxxiv + 426pp. 9 x 12.
22503-8 Paperbound $4.50

A HISTORY OF COSTUME, Carl Köhler. Definitive history, based on surviving pieces of clothing primarily, and paintings, statues, etc. secondarily. Highly readable text, supplemented by 594 illustrations of costumes of the ancient Mediterranean peoples, Greece and Rome, the Teutonic prehistoric period; costumes of the Middle Ages, Renaissance, Baroque, 18th and 19th centuries. Clear, measured patterns are provided for many clothing articles. Approach is practical throughout. Enlarged by Emma von Sichart. 464pp. 21030-8 Paperbound $3.50

ORIENTAL RUGS, ANTIQUE AND MODERN, Walter A. Hawley. A complete and authoritative treatise on the Oriental rug—where they are made, by whom and how, designs and symbols, characteristics in detail of the six major groups, how to distinguish them and how to buy them. Detailed technical data is provided on periods, weaves, warps, wefts, textures, sides, ends and knots, although no technical background is required for an understanding. 11 color plates, 80 halftones, 4 maps. vi + 320pp. 6⅛ x 9⅛. 22366-3 Paperbound $5.00

TEN BOOKS ON ARCHITECTURE, Vitruvius. By any standards the most important book on architecture ever written. Early Roman discussion of aesthetics of building, construction methods, orders, sites, and every other aspect of architecture has inspired, instructed architecture for about 2,000 years. Stands behind Palladio, Michelangelo, Bramante, Wren, countless others. Definitive Morris H. Morgan translation. 68 illustrations. xii + 331pp. 20645-9 Paperbound $3.00

THE FOUR BOOKS OF ARCHITECTURE, Andrea Palladio. Translated into every major Western European language in the two centuries following its publication in 1570, this has been one of the most influential books in the history of architecture. Complete reprint of the 1738 Isaac Ware edition. New introduction by Adolf Placzek, Columbia Univ. 216 plates. xxii + 110pp. of text. 9½ x 12¾. 21308-0 Clothbound $10.00

STICKS AND STONES: A STUDY OF AMERICAN ARCHITECTURE AND CIVILIZATION, Lewis Mumford. One of the great classics of American cultural history. American architecture from the medieval-inspired earliest forms to the early 20th century; evolution of structure and style, and reciprocal influences on environment. 21 photographic illustrations. 238pp. 20202-X Paperbound $2.00

THE AMERICAN BUILDER'S COMPANION, Asher Benjamin. The most widely used early 19th century architectural style and source book, for colonial up into Greek Revival periods. Extensive development of geometry of carpentering, construction of sashes, frames, doors, stairs; plans and elevations of domestic and other buildings. Hundreds of thousands of houses were built according to this book, now invaluable to historians, architects, restorers, etc. 1827 edition. 59 plates. 114pp. 7⅞ x 10¾. 22236-5 Paperbound $3.50

DUTCH HOUSES IN THE HUDSON VALLEY BEFORE 1776, Helen Wilkinson Reynolds. The standard survey of the Dutch colonial house and outbuildings, with constructional features, decoration, and local history associated with individual homesteads. Introduction by Franklin D. Roosevelt. Map. 150 illustrations. 469pp. 6⅝ x 9¼. 21469-9 Paperbound $4.00

JOHANN SEBASTIAN BACH, Philipp Spitta. One of the great classics of musicology, this definitive analysis of Bach's music (and life) has never been surpassed. Lucid, nontechnical analyses of hundreds of pieces (30 pages devoted to St. Matthew Passion, 26 to B Minor Mass). Also includes major analysis of 18th-century music. 450 musical examples. 40-page musical supplement. Total of xx + 1799pp.

(EUK) 22278-0, 22279-9 Two volumes, Clothbound $17.50

MOZART AND HIS PIANO CONCERTOS, Cuthbert Girdlestone. The only full-length study of an important area of Mozart's creativity. Provides detailed analyses of all 23 concertos, traces inspirational sources. 417 musical examples. Second edition. 509pp.

21271-8 Paperbound $3.50

THE PERFECT WAGNERITE: A COMMENTARY ON THE NIBLUNG'S RING, George Bernard Shaw. Brilliant and still relevant criticism in remarkable essays on Wagner's Ring cycle, Shaw's ideas on political and social ideology behind the plots, role of Leitmotifs, vocal requisites, etc. Prefaces. xxi + 136pp.

(USO) 21707-8 Paperbound $1.50

DON GIOVANNI, W. A. Mozart. Complete libretto, modern English translation; biographies of composer and librettist; accounts of early performances and critical reaction. Lavishly illustrated. All the material you need to understand and appreciate this great work. Dover Opera Guide and Libretto Series; translated and introduced by Ellen Bleiler. 92 illustrations. 209pp.

21134-7 Paperbound $2.00

HIGH FIDELITY SYSTEMS: A LAYMAN'S GUIDE, Roy F. Allison. All the basic information you need for setting up your own audio system: high fidelity and stereo record players, tape records, F.M. Connections, adjusting tone arm, cartridge, checking needle alignment, positioning speakers, phasing speakers, adjusting hums, trouble-shooting, maintenance, and similar topics. Enlarged 1965 edition. More than 50 charts, diagrams, photos. iv + 91pp.   21514-8 Paperbound $1.25

REPRODUCTION OF SOUND, Edgar Villchur. Thorough coverage for laymen of high fidelity systems, reproducing systems in general, needles, amplifiers, preamps, loudspeakers, feedback, explaining physical background. "A rare talent for making technicalities vividly comprehensible," R. Darrell, *High Fidelity*. 69 figures. iv + 92pp.   21515-6 Paperbound $1.25

HEAR ME TALKIN' TO YA: THE STORY OF JAZZ AS TOLD BY THE MEN WHO MADE IT, Nat Shapiro and Nat Hentoff. Louis Armstrong, Fats Waller, Jo Jones, Clarence Williams, Billy Holiday, Duke Ellington, Jelly Roll Morton and dozens of other jazz greats tell how it was in Chicago's South Side, New Orleans, depression Harlem and the modern West Coast as jazz was born and grew. xvi + 429pp.

21726-4 Paperbound $2.50

FABLES OF AESOP, translated by Sir Roger L'Estrange. A reproduction of the very rare 1931 Paris edition; a selection of the most interesting fables, together with 50 imaginative drawings by Alexander Calder. v + 128pp. 6½x9¼.

21780-9 Paperbound $1.50

THE ARCHITECTURE OF COUNTRY HOUSES, Andrew J. Downing. Together with Vaux's *Villas and Cottages* this is the basic book for Hudson River Gothic architecture of the middle Victorian period. Full, sound discussions of general aspects of housing, architecture, style, decoration, furnishing, together with scores of detailed house plans, illustrations of specific buildings, accompanied by full text. Perhaps the most influential single American architectural book. 1850 edition. Introduction by J. Stewart Johnson. 321 figures, 34 architectural designs. xvi + 560pp.

22003-6 Paperbound $4.00

LOST EXAMPLES OF COLONIAL ARCHITECTURE, John Mead Howells. Full-page photographs of buildings that have disappeared or been so altered as to be denatured, including many designed by major early American architects. 245 plates. xvii + 248pp. 7⅞ x 10¾.

21143-6 Paperbound $3.50

DOMESTIC ARCHITECTURE OF THE AMERICAN COLONIES AND OF THE EARLY REPUBLIC, Fiske Kimball. Foremost architect and restorer of Williamsburg and Monticello covers nearly 200 homes between 1620-1825. Architectural details, construction, style features, special fixtures, floor plans, etc. Generally considered finest work in its area. 219 illustrations of houses, doorways, windows, capital mantels. xx + 314pp. 7⅞ x 10¾.

21743-4 Paperbound $4.00

EARLY AMERICAN ROOMS: 1650-1858, edited by Russell Hawes Kettell. Tour of 12 rooms, each representative of a different era in American history and each furnished, decorated, designed and occupied in the style of the era. 72 plans and elevations, 8-page color section, etc., show fabrics, wall papers, arrangements, etc. Full descriptive text. xvii + 200pp. of text. 8⅜ x 11¼.

21633-0 Paperbound $5.00

THE FITZWILLIAM VIRGINAL BOOK, edited by J. Fuller Maitland and W. B. Squire. Full modern printing of famous early 17th-century ms. volume of 300 works by Morley, Byrd, Bull, Gibbons, etc. For piano or other modern keyboard instrument; easy to read format. xxxvi + 938pp. 8⅜ x 11.

21068-5, 21069-3 Two volumes, Paperbound $10.00

KEYBOARD MUSIC, Johann Sebastian Bach. Bach Gesellschaft edition. A rich selection of Bach's masterpieces for the harpsichord: the six English Suites, six French Suites, the six Partitas (Clavierübung part I), the Goldberg Variations (Clavierübung part IV), the fifteen Two-Part Inventions and the fifteen Three-Part Sinfonias. Clearly reproduced on large sheets with ample margins; eminently playable. vi + 312pp. 8⅛ x 11.

22360-4 Paperbound $5.00

THE MUSIC OF BACH: AN INTRODUCTION, Charles Sanford Terry. A fine, nontechnical introduction to Bach's music, both instrumental and vocal. Covers organ music, chamber music, passion music, other types. Analyzes themes, developments, innovations. x + 114pp.

21075-8 Paperbound $1.25

BEETHOVEN AND HIS NINE SYMPHONIES, Sir George Grove. Noted British musicologist provides best history, analysis, commentary on symphonies. Very thorough, rigorously accurate; necessary to both advanced student and amateur music lover. 436 musical passages. vii + 407 pp.

20334-4 Paperbound $2.75

MATHEMATICAL PUZZLES FOR BEGINNERS AND ENTHUSIASTS, Geoffrey Mott-Smith. 189 puzzles from easy to difficult—involving arithmetic, logic, algebra, properties of digits, probability, etc.—for enjoyment and mental stimulus. Explanation of mathematical principles behind the puzzles. 135 illustrations. viii + 248pp.

20198-8 Paperbound $1.75

PAPER FOLDING FOR BEGINNERS, William D. Murray and Francis J. Rigney. Easiest book on the market, clearest instructions on making interesting, beautiful origami. Sail boats, cups, roosters, frogs that move legs, bonbon boxes, standing birds, etc. 40 projects; more than 275 diagrams and photographs. 94pp.

20713-7 Paperbound $1.00

TRICKS AND GAMES ON THE POOL TABLE, Fred Herrmann. 79 tricks and games— some solitaires, some for two or more players, some competitive games—to entertain you between formal games. Mystifying shots and throws, unusual caroms, tricks involving such props as cork, coins, a hat, etc. Formerly *Fun on the Pool Table.* 77 figures. 95pp.

21814-7 Paperbound $1.00

HAND SHADOWS TO BE THROWN UPON THE WALL: A SERIES OF NOVEL AND AMUSING FIGURES FORMED BY THE HAND, Henry Bursill. Delightful picturebook from great-grandfather's day shows how to make 18 different hand shadows: a bird that flies, duck that quacks, dog that wags his tail, camel, goose, deer, boy, turtle, etc. Only book of its sort. vi + 33pp. 6½ x 9¼.   21779-5 Paperbound $1.00

WHITTLING AND WOODCARVING, E. J. Tangerman. 18th printing of best book on market. "If you can cut a potato you can carve" toys and puzzles, chains, chessmen, caricatures, masks, frames, woodcut blocks, surface patterns, much more. Information on tools, woods, techniques. Also goes into serious wood sculpture from Middle Ages to present, East and West. 464 photos, figures. x + 293pp.

20965-2 Paperbound $2.00

HISTORY OF PHILOSOPHY, Julián Marias. Possibly the clearest, most easily followed, best planned, most useful one-volume history of philosophy on the market; neither skimpy nor overfull. Full details on system of every major philosopher and dozens of less important thinkers from pre-Socratics up to Existentialism and later. Strong on many European figures usually omitted. Has gone through dozens of editions in Europe. 1966 edition, translated by Stanley Appelbaum and Clarence Strowbridge. xviii + 505pp.   21739-6 Paperbound $3.50

YOGA: A SCIENTIFIC EVALUATION, Kovoor T. Behanan. Scientific but non-technical study of physiological results of yoga exercises; done under auspices of Yale U. Relations to Indian thought, to psychoanalysis, etc. 16 photos. xxiii + 270pp.

20505-3 Paperbound $2.50

Prices subject to change without notice.
Available at your book dealer or write for free catalogue to Dept. GI, Dover Publications, Inc., 180 Varick St., N. Y., N. Y. 10014. Dover publishes more than 150 books each year on science, elementary and advanced mathematics, biology, music, art, literary history, social sciences and other areas.